Gleanings from the Book of Ruth

Dr. T.J. Reiser

PublishAmerica
Baltimore

© 2008 by Dr. T.J. Reiser.

All rights reserved. No part of this book may be reproduced, stored in a retrieval system or transmitted in any form or by any means without the prior written permission of the publishers, except by a reviewer who may quote brief passages in a review to be printed in a newspaper, magazine or journal.

First printing

ISBN: 1-60563-054-3
PUBLISHED BY PUBLISHAMERICA, LLLP
www.publishamerica.com
Baltimore

Printed in the United States of America

This book is dedicated to Richard and Lorraine's four children:
Lola, Bruce, Brian, and Lois.

FOREWORD

The individual responsible for the following material was a man by the name of Richard Schlupp. He was born in Canton, Ohio, became a Christian at age fifteen, and following high school he attended North Central Bible College in Minneapolis, Minnesota.

Richard was married, with four children, and lived in Verndale, Minnesota. He was an ordained minister with the Assemblies of God denomination and pastored churches in Palisade, Aitkin, and Motley, Minnesota. He spent most of his ministry as an evangelist and Bible teacher. Over the years he held services for over thirty different denominations, which took him from New York to Montana.

He was a multi-gifted person. Not only could he expound the Word of God in an excellent and memorable way, he also could play the piano and sing. In his personal life, he loved to cook and bake and loved visiting antique shops and flea markets, hunting for items to restore or share with others. Before his death in September of 1986, he was in the process of restoring his house in Verndale, Minnesota.

Despite his being away for evangelistic meetings, his heart was always at home. I know this because I was the Assembly of God pastor at Verndale from 1976-1979. During my short tenure there, "Brother Schlupp" (as I referred to him) became a great friend, colleague, and mentor. I always hoped that I could obtain some of his teaching material for my own ministry after he passed away, but it didn't seem like that would happen.

I moved from Verndale to Northfield, Minnesota and while there, I had Brother Schlupp for meetings a couple of times. It was during one of those meetings that Brother Schlupp did a study on the Book of Ruth. I had forgotten that I had taped those sessions until a few years ago. Doing some cleaning in the basement of the parsonage of our present ministry in Berlin, Wisconsin, I discovered those tapes!

To make a long story shorter, I have put those sessions on paper and trust that the material in this Book of Ruth will be of blessing to all who read it. I have put this together in his memory, with the hopes that Christ's name will be glorified.

My thanks to Brother Schlupp's daughter, Lola, for sending me some background information, as well as other notes from Brother Schlupp's teaching ministry. Also, I thank Elsie Deppe, our volunteer church secretary, for all her work at typing and retyping manuscripts.

—Terry Reiser

CHAPTER 1
Introduction—Ruth Is Deciding

We are looking at the Book of Ruth, which is the eighth book of the Old Testament, which is significant. But before we get into that, let me give you a New Testament reference to help us understand the Old Testament. Paul writes in 1 Corinthians 10:11, "These things happen to them as examples (types) and were written down as warnings for us, on whom the fulfillment of the ages has come."

If we can get this into our thinking, then we will know why we have the Old Testament. In the Old Testament their separation was in the flesh. They had to do everything always to the flesh. We are not separated in our flesh today; we are separated in our spirit. When our spirits get separated there will be a lot of things that we do and don't do because we are separated. Our activities change, our attitudes change, our behavior changes, our friends change quite often.

We are in the Book of Ruth, the eighth book of the Old Testament; it comes after Judges. We want to talk a little bit about what the setting was for this. If we are going to study something, it is important to look at the setting. In the first chapter Ruth is *deciding*. In the second chapter Ruth is *gleaning*. In the third chapter she is *resting*, and in the fourth and final chapter Ruth is *rewarded*. These are the things that come in our own experience.

We must first *decide*. Ruth is a very evangelical book. It is the most evangelical book in the Old Testament. It tells us we have to decide to serve the Lord. That sort of destroys some of our thinking doesn't it, because some say our parents brought us in. Well, there is no deciding in that, is there? Or some say the church brought us in. No, the church didn't bring us in, we had to decide to come in.

Then we *glean*. This is the work of the believer. He works. We were not saved to sit; we were saved to work and glean until the evening. Then we get to *rest*! Ruth got more for resting than she did for working. We sometimes think we've got to be busy and stir the bushes all the time, but we have to learn to rest at His feet also. We get more for resting than we do for gleaning, and then we're going to be *rewarded*!

Now, in this we will have a parenthesis here between these because of the "goel" (our "redeemer") and how he saved us, and we are going to take time to deal with this so that you understand. In fact, the Book of Ruth is the only place that our redeemer is talked about.

The author is unknown. No where do we find a place that tells us who wrote the Book of Ruth. The date is uncertain; there is no specific date that can be determined. In fact, if a scholar puts a date down, he puts a question mark with it because it is not really known when it was. It does tell us some things about this, and we will get to that. History and tradition does tell us that the author was Samuel, and this could be.

"Now it was in the days when the judges ruled." (That's the setting and time.) There were four hundred years in Israel's history when they did not have a king. They had no authority, there was no rule, and there was no restraint. Judges 17:6 says, "In those days there was no king in Israel, but every man did that which was right in his own eyes."

That verse shows us that there was no rule or restraint. When people do these things "that are right in their own eyes" it brings destruction to the earth. An example of this is the days of Noah. And we will have it again because of no rule or restraint.

God's people can get in this rut. They think that everyone ought to be allowed to do whatever they want to do; that will bring destruction. The 8th chapter, verse 1, finds the judges reiterating this. Let's find out what they did. "In those days there was no king in Israel: and in those days the tribe of the Danites sought them an inheritance to dwell in, for unto that day all their inheritance had not fallen unto them among the tribes of Israel." That tells us there was no king.

In the 19th chapter of Judges, verse 1, we have another verse that points out the fact there was no king. "And it came to pass in those days when there was no king in Israel, that there was a certain Levite sojourning on the side of Mount Ephraim, who took to him a concubine out of Bethlehem-Judah."

In the 21st chapter of Judges, verse 25, notice what it says: "In those days there was no king in Israel: for every man did that which was right in his own eyes." These are the verses that give us the setting and the times. There were lawless days under the judges. It was a democratic period, and Israel has some awful scenes. There was apostasy, there was backsliding, there was human failure, and there was violence.

In the darkest days, God works out his plan! That is what this book teaches us. You think we are living in dark days at the present, but remember, in the blackest days God is working out his plan. In the darkest days then God worked out his plan, and in our darkest days God wants to work out His plan!

Let's look at the two books, Joshua and Judges. Under Joshua there was victory, and there was joy. Why was this? It was because they were listening to God, and they were doing what He told them to do. There was communion and victory and joy, and there was obedience. These things all go together. To have victory one must be obedient. To have joy one must be in communion. This is the theme of the Book of Joshua, but when the children of Israel moved on down the line and some of the original people died off, we come to Judges.

Notice how it goes in the Book of Judges. The first thing you find is weeping, sorrow, defeat, and disobedience. You can clearly see the difference between these two books. The book we are studying does not come from the Joshua period; it comes from the Judges period when there was weeping, there was sorrow, there was defeat, and there was disobedience…and yet, God worked out his plan.

Much of this is seen in our world today; we have a Gideon and a Samson that move on the scene, and this is comparing to revival. In the midst of weeping and sorrow, defeat and disobedience, God can still work. He brings revival.

In the days of Martin Luther there was weeping, there was sorrow, there was defeat, and there was disobedience…and God sent a revival. In the days of the Wesley boys, there was weeping and sorrow, defeat and disobedience; great revival moved through the land. and God was moving by his Holy Spirit. It's a bright picture on a dark background!

Romans 5:20 is a good verse to compare to these things that we have before us: "But where sin abounded, grace did much more abound." It is a bright picture on a dark background, and you know how beautiful that is. Think of a painting with a dark background, then several bright colors are added; isn't it beautiful? The artist begins with old dark chalk on a parchment or canvas and you think, "What is going to become of this?" The next thing you know there's a beautiful white house, a river, a ship, and everything is beautiful, and it all came out of the dark background! In our dark backgrounds today, we have a picture of grace.

Before we continue, I want to remind you that Ruth is the eighth book. "Eight" signifies a new beginning. Every number in the Bible means something, and "eight" is a new beginning. We are really in the day of rest; we are children of God living in the darkness while waiting for the morning to come. We are waiting for the eighth day. There will be a new beginning when the eighth day comes. We are resting from our labors. This is the rest that causes the weary to rest, and this is the refreshing, "With stammering lips in another tongue, I'll speak unto this people." We are living in the seventh day, and we're waiting for morning to come.

Now there were a lot of things in the Bible that were eight. Perhaps you don't remember them all, so I have made the following list:

- Resurrection is the eighth day; the first day of the week.
- circumcision came on the eighth day.
- Noah was the eighth person.
- Sunday is the eighth day.
- David was the eighth son.

We're taking about the eighth book; a new beginning. God is about to do something different.

Ruth was called out by God. She is mentioned with four other women in the genealogy of Christ. Turn to Matthew 1:6. There we see Ruth in the genealogy of Jesus. The four women in the genealogy were all terrible women with bad backgrounds.

Mary, we all know, was highly favored by God. Ruth was called out by God as we see in verse 5 of the genealogy: "And Salmon begat Boaz of Rachab; and Boaz begat Obed of Ruth; and Obed begat Jesse." This is the Ruth we are studying about.

God took a Moabitess from the cursed nation of the Moabite. The Moabites came into being when Lot had an affair with his own daughter, a thing that God detests. Out of the loins of a man that was disobedient to God came the Moabites, and God cursed them. He told the children of Israel to not have anything to do with the Moabites, and now God takes a little Moabite girl and brings her into the family, and from her comes our Savior.

Can't we see ourselves in this? God called us out of nothing. Our background was bad (before we accepted Christ); we were sinners. We were as the Moabites, detested, but God changed us through Christ. We don't rejoice over where we came from; we rejoice over where we're going. God is not interested in where we've been, only where we're going.

Genesis 19:37 tells us God had to curse the Moabites because of the illicit union between Lot and his daughter because they thought that no seed was going to come due to the destruction. Verse 36 says, "Thus were both the daughters of Lot with child by their father." Notice verse 37, "The firstborn bare a son and called his name Moab; the same is the father of the Moabites unto this day."

In Psalms, we read "Moab is my wash pot." And that is what is referred to in Genesis 19:36, 37; it tells us where Moab came from. So, if you wonder why God is getting Elimelech into trouble, it is because he went to Moab. This is why they went from Judah—which means "praise"—to a wash pot.

The Book of Ruth begins (verse 1) with, "Now it came to pass in the days when the judges ruled, that there was a famine in the land. And a certain man of Bethlehem Judah went to sojourn in the country of Moab, he and his wife, and his two sons." Now, let's analyze this. There was a famine in the land. Famines bring tests and trials. The land of Canaan was to be a land of blessing and promise. There were to be grapes, and milk, and honey. The church is to be a place of sustenance, of life, of living water. If it ceases to be this, there is a problem. One can either run back to the mess they came out of, or look up and ask God for help. Here they were, in a famine, and instead of sticking by the goods, he runs…and notice, he took his family with him!

Apply that to your own life. When you sin or backslide, you always take someone with you. When you run out on things, you usually take someone with you. And so, the "certain man of Bethlehem-Judah went to sojourn in the country of Moab," and who does he take with him? His wife and two sons. The name of the "certain man" was Elimelech!

Names mean something; Elimelech means "my God is King" and he isn't going to act like it. Our name is "Christian" and we don't always act like it.

Every Old Testament name has a meaning, and if you want to get some spiritual things out of the Old Testament, take these names and study them. Elimelech means "My God is King," but instead of God being his king, we find him running back to Moab. He's running to a heathen nation for help! Let me tell you, we've got a God who owns the cattle on a thousand hills and the wealth in every mine. He can supply all of your needs according to His riches in glory; there's nothing too difficult for Him. He is Jehovah-Jireh, the Great Provider. When you have God helping you, you and God are a majority, and you don't need anyone but God to help.

The name of Elimelech's wife was Naomi. The word "Naomi" means "lovely, gracious, a pleasant one," but she was subject unto her husband, so she went to Moab. The names of the two sons are Mahlon and Chilion. They are Ephraimites of Bethlehem-Judah (house of bread and plenty, and Judah means "praise"). They came from a good place but they "came into the country of Moab, and they continued there."

Look at what they attached to Mahlon. You can generally tell what kind of an attitude some people have by what comes out of their mouth. Just think of what they attached to this kid: "sickly, weak, and unable." This somewhat depicts how Elimelech felt about God…"my God is King," but he names his child "weak, sickly, and unable."

Then we have Chilion, and his name means, "tiny one, wasting away, and sad." This really shows what Elimelech was feeling. No wonder he ran! What do we do when we're sad and wasting away? We run! The spiritual lesson to learn here is to run to God, stand still, look up, see the salvation of your God!

Moving on to verse 3, "Elimelech, Naomi's husband died and she was left, and her two sons." There is a teaching today that says once you are a believer God will always bring you back. This verse, however, shows that he didn't come back. He died. He ran, and died in Moab. Look at Lot, Jonah, the Prodigal son; they were not fruitful in a strange place. Was Jonah fruitful in the belly of the whale? No. Was Lot fruitful in the cave? No. Was the Prodigal son fruitful in the pig pen? No; he lost everything. Some of these came back: Jonah came back and got a second chance. Lot died there. Elimelech dies in Moab.

Notice that the trip to Moab did not pay off as they expected—neither did Jonah's trip. Naomi says, "I went out full, and I came home empty." This is what happens when we don't run to God for our source of help. We seek entertainment or anything that might satisfy. When some folks lose their mate they think they have got to find someone, and they grab the first one that comes along. They don't read in the Scriptures, "Marriage is to be honorable in the Lord." (Hebrews 13:4). They should have someone who loves the Lord, but they settle for less. Our choices really determine what we're going to have.

So, "Elimelech, Naomi's husband died, and she was left and her two sons. And they took them wives of the women of Moab" (vs. 3, 4). This is a clear picture of how children are affected. This man went to Moab, he went to the heathen for help, and now his kids are going to get hooked up with them. You may say, "Everything turned out okay," but you can't just look at how it turned out; you must also see that God doesn't will everything for us that happens to us. Prayer changes things. Our choices change things. We can change things if we want to.

"They took them wives of the women of Moab." The name of one was Orpah, and the name of the other Ruth; and they dwelt there about ten years" (vs. 4). You see, they were only going to make a short trip, be there long enough for the famine to come to an end, and they stayed ten years! In ten years the man lost his life, and his kids married heathen girls.

Now the girl's names have meaning also. Orpah means "double-mindedness or unstable." This really is a picture of what she was. She was very double-minded. She was blind—the Hebrew word can be translated "blind." What does James tell us about being unstable? "A double-minded man is unstable in all his ways. "Ruth" means "rose." Ruth is a rose, and satisfied.

Verse 5 tells us that "Mahlon and Chilion died also, both of them; and the woman was bereft of her two sons and her husband. Then she arose with her daughters-in-law that she might return from the country of Moab, for she had heard in the country of Moab how that the Lord had visited His people in giving them bread." Naomi said, I've got to get out of Moab and get home!

So Naomi said to her daughters-in-law, "Go, return each to her mother's house; the Lord deal kindly with you as ye have dealt with the dead, and with me." They didn't even know the Lord, and now she's asking the Lord to be kind to them. He is, and He's wanting to bring them out of this land.

Naomi said to her daughters-in-law, "you go." Then in verse 9, "the Lord grant you that ye may find rest, each of you in the house of her husband." How can you find rest when you don't know the One who gives it? How can we go to the unsaved and put our hands in theirs and say, "Oh, my dear one, have rest." They will have no rest until they know Jesus. The world is not at rest. They don't know what this rest is, but Naomi desires "rest for each of you in the house of the husband." She is then filled with emotion and kissed them, "and they lifted up their voice and wept."

We need to start crying over the right things. We can't weep and be moved with emotion and tomorrow do the same foolish, silly thing all over again. Our tears have to move us to repentance.

Verse 10: "And they said unto her, 'Surely we will return with thee unto thy people.'" In other words, we're going to go with you. There was a turning point here. God doesn't work with multitudes; He works with individuals. He went to the woman at the well. He went to Nicodemus. Was He the only preacher in the church? No, there were lots of them, but he went to one. So He'll come to one!

Naomi said, "Turn again, my daughters: Why will ye go with me? Are there yet any more sons in my womb that they may be your husbands?" That was an earthly thing to bring up...an old, gray-haired woman and now she's talking about babies? (vs. 12). "Turn again, my daughters, go your way; for I am too old to have an husband. If I should say, I have hope, if I should have an husband also tonight, and should also bear sons [vs. 13] would you tarry for them till they are grown? Would you stay for them from having husbands? Nay, my daughters; for it grieveth me much for your sakes that the hand of the Lord is gone out against me."

Now if there is any "haywire doctrine" in the book of Ruth, there it is. Who walked out? Did God walk out? No sir! Don't you get into hot water and say it's the Lord's doings. Do you blame your trouble on God? God's done everything to get you out of trouble. This is the personal testimony of a backslider...they blame God, yet God had grace to bring them back. So we don't quote this verse to show that God is mad at us. He isn't mad at us; He has grace to bring us back.

"I went out full, and the Lord hath brought me home again empty: why then call ye me, Naomi, seeing the Lord hath testified against me and the Almighty hath afflicted me?" That's "haywire doctrine."

"So Naomi returned and Ruth the Moabitess, her daughters-in-law with her, which returned out of the country of Moab: and they came to Bethlehem in the beginning of barley harvest." Do you know what Israel is celebrating at barley harvest? The Passover Feast. Blood was on the lintils and door posts, and Naomi came home to Father's house. That's when we come home—when the blood was applied to the lintils and door posts. The backslider came home when the blood was applied; Naomi came home.

Look at several decisions that we have from Ruth. She renounced her people and her past life. She wanted to lodge and have communion with God's people. She wanted separation. "For where you go, I am going" (1 Peter 1:8). "Thy [personal pronoun] God shall be my God." This is what we all need to do; everyone needs this experience. They need to have the God of heaven and earth become their God. There needs to be consecration—she consecrated herself.

Resurrection—the son that she bare was more than life to Naomi. This is true of our Savior. He has brought us new life again. So, these are the six decisions from chapter 1.

Some additional truths from chapter 1: Naomi means blessed. Mara means bitter. She blames God, but His only endeavor was to bring her back. She arrived at the right place; she came at the time of barley harvest—the Passover. It was in the month of April that the barley harvest took place and she came. Her sins were forgiven. What happens at Passover? (1) Sins are forgiven. (2) All things become new. (3) Complete forgiveness and restoration…this is when Naomi came home. What do we get when we come home to our Fathers house? Our sins forgiven, all things become new, we have complete forgiveness. What should God forgive for us? Everything. Complete forgiveness and then He restores us…restoration!

When Adam and Eve sinned they were turned upside down. Their spirit was on top in the creation. God willed that the spirit of man be on top, but when they sinned their body (flesh) came on top. You and I were created in sin and shaped in iniquity, and our body was on top. Remember how you pamper your body, and baby it, and see what all you could get to thrill it and make it feel good? We've been turned upside down. We're not really upside down; we're right side up! The new man is on top and we're no longer doing things that please the flesh, for the flesh is going to die. It's going to the grave, but we're pleasing the new man that is within us. This is what happens in Passover. There is a restoration. We've been restored. The world thinks we're odd. They think we're religious fanatics, but we've just been turned right side up.

"I went out," Naomi says in these verses. She took her own life in her hands. The sheep go out but the Shepherd brings them back home. That's a wonderful name, "home." There are some privileges in the home: an open cupboard, people who love you. "The Lord hath brought me home again" (vs. 21).

There are special liberties in your home: an open cupboard or a refrigerator; it's a place of rest—there's security there. There is love. Bitter dealings brought her home. I ask the question of you, "What will it take to bring you home? God often uses some unique situations to bring us home. Look at all the woman went through to bring her home. She was obedient to that "thing" she was married to, and he dragged her off. It took 10 years of hell to bring her home; but she came home!

REVIEW QUESTIONS FOR CHAPTER 1

1. Ruth is the eighth book of the Old Testament. What is the significance of the number eight?
2. What nation did Ruth come from? What is so significant about that?
3. The Book of Ruth takes place during what period? Why is this important?
4. In chapter 1, Ruth is deciding. What does that mean?
5. What do the following names mean?
   (a) Elimelech
   (b) Mahlon and Chilion
   (c) Orpah and Ruth
   (d) Naomi

CHAPTER 2
Ruth Is Gleaning

In chapter 1 we saw Ruth deciding. We must decide. We are not born into the Kingdom of God as babies. We are not brought in by our family. Our church doesn't bring us in. Each must decide.

Chapter 2's heading is "Ruth Gleaning." After we accept Christ as our Savior we come to the fields of the Lord, and there is work to be done. He did not save us to rest. We've entered into rest; the "rest" we have today is a rest in the Holy Spirit, and after we have this rest we work.

Naomi had a kinsman (v. 1). This is like saying I have a Savior in New Testament talk. You see, New Testament talk and Old Testament talk are two different things. Before the Savior came, they talked about His coming. They weren't too evangelical in their thinking, but if we are going to put verse 1 of chapter 2 in New Testament talk today, Naomi said, "I have a Savior. I have one that can help me out of my pickle—out of my dilemma; I have a Savior." Do you remember who helped you out of your problems? A Savior, right?

Please notice here that she didn't say, "I have a hero." Is Jesus a hero? No, we don't call Him a hero, we call Him a Redeemer. I have a redeemer. The word "kinsman" can be translated "redeemer." Kinsman is an interesting word. We really do not use this word that much. Another Hebrew word for "kinsman" is "redeemer." The song says, "I will sing of my Redeemer and His wondrous love to me," but we could sing, "I will sing of my Kinsman..." because Jesus became our relative, didn't He? How did He do this? He took upon Himself the flesh of Adam, He became a Redeemer for us. You're going to hear about this so much that you'll dream about it at night. So, it isn't a hero here, it's a redeemer, and He's the Eternal One.

A verse that substantiates this is 2 Corinthians 8:9, "For you know the grace of our Lord Jesus Christ, that though He was rich, yet for your sakes

He became poor, that you, through his poverty might be rich." [The logos needs to become Ramah, living.] This is more than money in the First National Bank! As soon as we think of rich, we think of money in one's pocketbook, but Jesus has done more for us than put money in our pocketbook. "And He, through His poverty made us rich." He left the portals of heaven, He laid aside His glory, He laid aside all the wealth and the beauties of heaven and took on Himself poverty. By that He was born in the stable. He didn't even have money to pay His taxes. He emptied Himself of all these things that through that poverty you and I might be made sons and daughters of God.

Notice in this verse it says, "A mighty man of wealth." Do you know this is not mentioned in any of the other sixty-six books? It's a beautiful piece. A mighty man of wealth—Boaz. This word, Boaz, means "son of strength." The name, Jesus, means "Savior." This word, Boaz, is a son of strength. This is one of the names of the pillars in the temple. 1 Kings 7:21 and 2 Chronicles 3:16, tells us that one of the pillars in the temple was called "Boaz." Who are we? We are the temple of the Holy Spirit. We need some pillars too, and it would be good to have the son of strength for that's what Jesus is to us. You see, Boaz, now in our story, is a picture of Jesus.

The mighty man of wealth took on himself a poor little Moabitess that was cast out. He's going to marry her. Who's going to marry us? Jesus! The mighty Savior of the world is going to marry the Church. Isn't that great! The Old Testament shows us this.

Poor Naomi, stricken family, allied to powerful Boaz. Here's little Naomi…can't you see her coming home? They say, "Is this Naomi?" She said, "Don't call me that, I'm Mara: for the Almighty hath dealt very bitterly with me." (1:20)

Then she found out she had a relative who could bring her in. She said she was going to ally herself with him. I'm going to go over and take what he's got. That's what Jesus wants us to do. That's why He became related to us—to give us everything He's got! Why don't you take it? Quit acting so foolish. God doesn't want us to feel lost and undone; He wants to bring us in and make us heirs to everything God's got!

Remember Elimelech? When his stomach was empty he ran to the heathen for help. Let me ask you a question even though there is probably no answer. Why did Elimelech go to the heathen for help when Boaz lived in the camp? Do you know that Elimelech could have gotten help from Boaz—after all, he was his next of kin. Instead, he ran to the heathen. That reminds me of Christians who say I don't have anyone to help me…got to go to the pig pen and get some. Why don't you go to Boaz?

See how foolish this is? Can you see yourself in this? This is just how foolish we are. We have help right where we are, but we have to run. Elimelech had help at home but he died among the heathen. This should show us something. Why did he go? It's our foolish nature. We have to learn that in our dilemmas we always look up—never around us.

The word "Moabitess" is mentioned five times in this chapter. It sort of stirs one up that they have to keep bringing up where she came from. This is the way people are. Ruth, the sinner. Five times they bring this up in this chapter. They want to tell—or make sure—that they tell she's a Moabitess. This is God's people talking. "Now don't you call me a sinner…I was a sinner, I'm not a sinner now; I'm a saint because I've been forgiven." That helps our self-image!

Now, the reward of faith begins (vs. 2), ears of corn during the barley harvest. They came in the daily harvest. When we hear "ears of corn" we think she's taking roasting ears off of the stalk. She's not doing that, she's gleaning grain in the field, what we call "small grain." "And her hap was to light on a part of the field belonging to Boaz, who was of the kindred of Elimelech" (vs. 3). "Hap" can actually be translated "luck." Is there luck with God? No, "All things work together for good to them who love the Lord" (Romans 8:28).

The poor Moabitess was defeated and hated afar off. She was under the curse of the Law. She gleans; she's treated as a beggar. Look at Leviticus 23:22 and notice the law of gleaning. This is for the strangers and the poor. Notice what it says, "When ye reap the harvest of your land, thou shalt not make clear riddance of the corners of thy field when thou reapest, neither shall thou gather any gleaning of thy harvest: thou shalt leave them unto the poor and to the stranger. I am the Lord your God."

That was the rule. They couldn't have square corners in the field, they had to make them round and they had to leave those pieces. If you dropped anything on the ground you weren't allowed to pick it up, and then the poor came behind. Do you realize the kind of an attitude this would make for people? If you don't have these things in your heart you would get a little vexed with this, so these reapers weren't very kind to the strangers and beggars who came behind them. They were detested. They were not appreciated. Do you appreciate people who don't work for what they get?

Naomi could have gone to the field but she sent Ruth because she was young. You see, Naomi is older now—the girl (Ruth) is treated as a beggar. She's treated roughly, and she's never had to take this route before. They are two destitute widows. They were at the end of their rope with a knot tied in it. Do you realize that widows in those days died because of lack of sustenance? There was no Social Security or Aid to Dependent Children, or any of these things. But you see, God always makes a way.

Now Ruth is guided. Look at verse 3; it says, "She went and came, and gleaned in the field after the reapers: and her hap was to light on a part of the field belonging unto Boaz, who was of the kindred of Elimelech." Ruth was guided. The fields were not separated by hedges. There were landmarks (heaps of stones), and it happened to her to be on this portion of the field. Ruth's life—her entire life—turned at this point. It seems like chance, but it was God; the clear shaping of her course by unseen hands guided by God to a certain field.

Do you think you are where you are because of luck? No, God guided you. You're not who you are today by luck, but God is molding and shaping you in the place where you are. The steps of a righteous man are ordered of the Lord. You see, you are in this field—great issues arise from small incidences. Ruth could have been guided to a more godly family in those godless days but "everyone was doing everything that was right in their own eyes." There was no restraint. It was a wicked thing, and God takes a little Moabitess that doesn't know A from B, doesn't know beans from peas, but she says, I'm going with you. She comes and God guides her to the most godly field...that's the Lord.

Look at the Book of Esther, chapter 6, verse 1. "On that night, could not the king sleep, and he commanded to bring the book of records of the Chronicles; and they were read before the king." Do you know what happened because the king couldn't sleep? The Jewish nation was saved. They would have been annihilated if the king hadn't had the Chronicles read. And he had them read because he couldn't sleep!

We often say, "Oh, dear God, I can't get to sleep...I need some Tylenol. I've got to take something and be put out." Don't get worked up over not being able to sleep. It saved the Jewish nation, and it might save you! God just may be in this thing! I mention this because little things can mean something bigger on down the road.

Here's Ruth, all these fields...the whole outfit, fields all over, only piles of rock...and she gets out there and starts picking up and gleaning along the way, and she lands right in Boaz's field. Isn't it marvelous how God guides?

The paragraph changes now in verse 4 of chapter 2. "Behold Boaz came from Bethlehem and said unto the reaper, 'The Lord be with you.' And they answered him, 'The Lord bless thee.'" That's capital and labor...there's never a strike. God is dealing with a stranger of the Gentiles. In the Catholic Church, I like it when one of the priests calls out and says, "The Lord be with you" and he is answered back, "And also with you." I'm reminded of that when I read this verse.

The boss (Boaz) greeted his workers, "The Lord be with you." You see, he asked the Lord to be with them and in turn the workers asked the Lord to bless him. We don't always feel like this about our boss; he's considered an "old tight wad" or "money hungry." You think, "He's going to take all the life out of me, and what am I going to get for it?" What would your boss think if you walked in and said, "The Lord bless you." And if your boss would answer you, "And the Lord be with you," some people would lose their teeth! This is a beautiful thing to see. This is to be our attitude; this is the way Boaz was.

"Then said Boaz unto his servant that was set over the reapers, whose damsel is this?" (vs. 5). Don't you want Jesus to take note of you? You see, Boaz is a picture of Jesus. And who did he notice? All the workers, but he said, "Whose damsel is this?" If only Jesus (Boaz) sees me.

The charm of her presence! She was poor, but he noticed her. This is also a picture of life in the church. We are to care for the young converts who have come from Moab. We are to care for the young converts that come from Moab! God wants us to look at them and do something for them. There's a good sermon here on caring for the young converts.

Boaz saw and heard of her devotion, and she found grace in his sight. Notice verse 6, "And the servant that was set over the reapers answered and said, "It is the Moabitish damsel that came back with Naomi out of the country of Moab." (There it is, this Moab thing. They brought it up twice now in this chapter, and we've got three more times to go.) But notice, she found grace in his sight.

The word "Moabite appears five times. "Five" in the word of God has a lesson for us also. Five in the word of God is the number of grace. Here are some places where the word five appears:

> • David had five stones.
> • Exodus 13:18 says, "but God led the people about through the way of the wilderness of the Red Sea: and the children of Israel went up harnessed out of the land of Egypt." The word "harnessed" comes from a Hebrew word that means they came out five in a rank. Five is the number of grace and they came out/through the Red Sea five in a rank!
> • The Brazen Altar where our sins were dealt with in the Old Testament was five cubits square…again, the number of grace.
> • In 1 Corinthians 1:27, 28, there are five classes that God deals with. They are, "foolish things, weak things, lowly things, despised things, and things that are not." In the King James Version, it's not quite as clear, but it says, "But God hath chosen the foolish things of the world to confound the wise; and God hath chosen the weak things of the world to confound the things which are mighty; and these things of the world and the things which are despised, hath God chosen, yea, and the things which are not to bring to naught things that are."

You see in verse 26 He says, "For you see your calling, brethren [that's believers] how that not many wise men after the flesh, not many mighty, not many noble," are called. He didn't call that type of people; He called foolish and weak, and lowly and despised, and those that think they are nothing. So when you hear a bunch of horn blowing about where they've come from, don't pay any attention because it doesn't make any difference. The grace of Boaz brought Ruth into the royal line.

Ruth the Moabitess is mentioned five times, and you see God dealing with her. We were sinners, and five is a very important number to us, for grace brought us into the Kingdom of God.

Let's look at verses 7 and 8. "And she said, 'I pray you, let me glean and gather after the reapers among the sheaves." You see, she spoke up! Here's a little hint…if you want your Boaz to do something, speak up! You may say, "Oh, the Lord knows what I need." Get off that holy thing you're on…He wants to hear you say you need it. You've got to tell Him what you want.

Ruth could have said, "O dear, there's the mighty man of God. I don't dare tell him what I need." Don't start that way. Speak up! Ruth the Moabitess did; she spoke right up. They were poverty stricken, and she said, "I pray you, let me glean and gather after the reapers among the sheaves: so she came, and that continued even from the morning until now, that she tarried a little in the house." Then said Boaz unto Ruth, "Hearest thou not, my daughter? Go not to glean in another field, neither go from hence, but abide here fast by my maidens." Stay right here, don't go to another field that's regulated by me…that's pretty good advice for us too. We don't need to go to Buddah's field, Islam's field, or anyone else; we're in the Lord's field. Verse 8 states, "abide fast here," or "here fast by my maidens." Fast here is translated as glued. That's determination…something will happen.

Look at verse 9: "Let thine eyes be on the field that they do not reap, and go thou after them: have I not charged the young men that they shall not touch thee? And when thou are athirst, go unto the vessels and drink of that which the young men have drawn." We can correlate this with the living water. God never promised to bless our head; He wants to bless our heart. People don't come into the kingdom through their head, they come with their heart!

There was safety in the Lord's field. Boaz commanded the young not to touch her, and when she is thirsty to go to the vessel. Notice how grateful she was about all this. She found a place at his house and at his table. We've found a place at the Lord's table. He has invited us in. We're to eat there forever!

Think of Mephibosheth in 2 Samuel, chapter 9. You remember he was lame, he had lost his walking ability through a fall. We lost ours through one, too! The nurse dropped him and he was lame, but when he was invited to King David's house he said, "You eat everyday at my table." And as long as he is at the table his lameness didn't show.

You can't tell who is lame at the table. Sometimes we are all a little lame. We don't walk like we should, but pull up to the table and eat. Our lameness doesn't show when we sit at the table. Folks look around and say, "These Christians are no different than we are." Christians aren't perfect; they've just been forgiven. So it says, "There was a place at his table." You go to the vessels and drink what the young man had drawn, and in verse 14, you are supposed to eat at the table.

Then notice in verse 10, "she fell on her face and bowed herself to the ground." She was grateful. How grateful are you that you found a place at His table? We are to be ever grateful and thank Him every day for it. Fall on your face, bow yourself before him, and say, "Lord, I'm thankful that I'm eating at your table. I wasn't worthy but you made me worthy."

Continuing with verse 10, "And she said to him, why have I found grace in thine eyes, that thou shouldst take knowledge of me, seeing I am a stranger?" That is to be our attitude as well. Lord, why did you choose me? Ruth was grateful. There was grace here...and kindness.

"And Boaz answered and said unto her, it hath fully been showed me, all that thou has done unto thy mother-in-law since the death of thine husband: and how thou hast left thy father and thy mother, and the land of the nativity, and come out unto a people which thou knewest not heretofore. The Lord recompense thy work and a full reward be given thee of the Lord God of Israel, under whose wings thou art come to trust." That is my prayer for you who are reading these words, that the Lord will fully reward you because you have come under his reign.

"Then she said, let me find favor in thy sight, my Lord; for that thou hast comforted me, and for that thou hast spoken friendly unto thine handmaid, though I be not like unto one of thine handmaidens." You see, we all have hang-ups. Don't look at the other handmaids and say they're not acting like us. Notice these words, "friendly unto thine handmaid." The Hebrew rendering here is "He spoke to the heart of the handmaid." Please note that he doesn't speak much to the brain and the intellect, but he speaks to the heart! What did the Lord speak to in you? He spoke to your heart—that's the real you inside.

"Boaz said unto her" (in verse 14), "at mealtime come thou hither, and eat of the bread." If any man eat of that bread he will never hunger. Oh, the bread at the table! Doesn't it satisfy you? Boaz continues, "...dip thy morsel in the vinegar. And she sat beside the reapers and he reached her parched corn and she did eat and it sufficed her." There is satisfaction at the table. When you eat at the Lord's table, you're satisfied.

Verse 15 says, "and when she was risen up to glean, Boaz commanded his young men saying, let her glean even among the sheaves and reproach her not." The word "reproach" in the Hebrew means "shame her not." (Verse 16:) "And let fall also some of the handfuls of purpose for her, and leave them that she may glean them, and rebuke her not."

The Lord does drop some handfuls of purpose for us; we're to let a little bit fall from us also. A quote I have noted is, "That that I kept, I lost; but what I've given I still have." I try to live by that. If you eat from this [spiritual] table and keep it to yourself, you'll lose it, but if you go and share, you'll still have it. That's just the way God works. Teach a Sunday School class, open up your home and give out what you have. It doesn't matter if you think your best is good enough or not; the Lord says it's good enough. That's all that matters!

"So she gleaned in the field until even, and beat out that she had gleaned, and it was about an ephah of barley" (verse 17). That's a bushel and three pints! She did pretty well! That was a pretty heavy load to carry home. "And she took it up [that's the bushel and three pints] and went into the city: and her mother-in-law saw what she had gleaned; and she brought forth and gave to her that she had reserved after she was sufficed." (Verse 19:) "And her mother-in-law said unto her, where hast thou gleaned today?" (In other words, "Where did you work?") "And where wroughtest thou? Blessed be he that did take knowledge of thee. And she showed her mother-in-law with whom she had wrought, and said, the man's name with whom I wrought today is Boaz. And Naomi said unto her daughter-in-law, blessed be he of the Lord, who hath not left off his kindness to the living and to the dead. And Naomi said unto her, The man is near of kin unto us, one of our next kinsmen."

I want you to notice what she did. I've made a note of some things that God spoke to me about in this study. She left the straw and took the wheat home. Some sermons have more straw than wheat—beat out the wheat, take it home and leave the straw on the church floor! If you get one grain, take it; take the wheat home! Ruth beat the wheat and took home what could help her and sustain her and left the straw. She left the worthless part. 1

Corinthians 15:58 says, "We labor not in vain in the Lord." That's a New Testament verse that helps us here.

Notice that Ruth returns with a supply to Naomi. She took what he gave her. Also notice in verse 17 that "she gleaned in the field until even and beat out that she had gleaned, and it was an ephah of barley." And she said to him, this is way too much. I'm sure you are going to go to the poor house over giving me so much! I'll give you back part of what I got. No, it doesn't say that. We take what He gives us. Don't worry about Him being poor; He became poor so we could become rich. He brought us into an inheritance from the man that loves us and is our Father, who owns the cattle on a thousand hills and the wealth in every mine. Ruth took what he gave her.

Naomi said, "Where did you work today? Where did you get all this?" Ruth said, the man's name is Boaz. This rich, strong redeemer is related to Naomi's dead husband—a blood relative. The barley harvest, the wheat harvest, is Passover and Pentecost…we'll have more about that.

Here's the discovery! Naomi, the stricken relative of the dead family saw hope for the dead as well as the living in the kinsman redeemer. "Naomi said unto her daughter-in-law, Blessed be he of the Lord who hath not left off his kindness to the living and to the dead. And Naomi said unto her, the man is near of kin unto us, one of our next kinsmen."

Now turn to 1 Thessalonians 4:13-14. "But I would not have you to be ignorant, brethren, concerning those which are asleep [dead]; that ye sorrow not, even as others which have not hope. For if we believe that Jesus died and rose again, even so them also which sleep in Jesus will God bring with Him." He's the God of the living and the dead. Verses 15-16: "For this we say unto you by the Word of the Lord that we which are alive and remain unto the coming of the Lord shall not prevent them which are asleep. For the Lord Himself shall descend from heaven with a shout, with the voice of the archangel, and with the trump of God; and the dead in Christ shall rise first." He's the God of the living and the dead!

In Ruth 2:20 it says, "He hasn't left off his kindness to the living and the dead." Who is Naomi referring to? Boaz. And who is Boaz in our story? Jesus! Jesus remembers us whether we go to Him by the grave or living and caught up in the air—all of us will be with the Lord. "Comfort one another (1 Thessalonians 4) with these words." The coming of the Lord is to be a comfort to us.

The tables are turned; God's hand is not against her now. She kept fast to the redeemer until the end. See, she's getting her doctrine straightened up. "And Ruth the Moabitess," there it is for the fifth time now, "said, He said unto me also, thou shalt keep fast by my young men until they have ended all my harvest. And Naomi said unto Ruth, her daughter-in-law, it is good, my daughter, that thou go out with his maidens, that they meet thee not in any other field."

Now she's finally getting straightened up. Yesterday she was sending her to heathen gods. Now she says you had better stick fast to him. The backslider is getting turned around, getting her values straight. Verse 23: "So she kept fast by the maidens of Boaz to glean unto the end of barley harvest, and of wheat harvest, and dwelt with her mother-in-law."

Now, what does this really say? In New Testament language, what does this say? "She abideth through barley harvest and wheat harvest." She stayed in the field from Passover to Pentecost. There are 50 days between these two events, and she came to Pentecost. We've had Easter and Passover, and in 50 days we will have Pentecost. Again, what does this say in New Testament language? Get saved, get under the blood, get your sins forgiven, but please abide in the field until you receive power after that the Holy Ghost is come upon you" (Acts 1:8). Stay in the field and get the whole ball of wax…get the whole thing!

It doesn't say she stayed there for Passover and decided to lay off for Pentecost. We have some that want to do that. "I don't know that the baptism is so essential." You don't know the Word of God; that's what's wrong, and you don't know what God wants to do. You can't do a thing until you're anointed. Jesus was anointed. He said, "The Spirit of the Lord is upon me because I was born of the Virgin Mary." *No*, he did not say that. He said, "The Spirit of the Lord is upon me (Luke 4:18) because I have been anointed." When did He get anointed? When he stood in the Jordan River and was baptized by John the Baptist. When He came up out of the water the Spirit of the Lord descended upon Him and He was baptized in the Holy Spirit.

Acts 10:38 (later preaching in the house of Cornelius), if you get this into your thinking, you'll see that you are supposed to stay in the field from Passover to Pentecost. You don't leave the field! Who did God anoint?

Jesus of Nazareth. Jesus is His earthly name; lots of boys were named Jesus in His day. The Jews quit using Jesus for a name when He was crucified on the cross. Joshua is the Hebrew rendering. Nazareth was his home town. This man was anointed with the Holy Ghost and with power…and notice what he did with it. It says he was anointed with the Holy Ghost and with power, and he went about doing good. Doing good! And he healed all that were oppressed of the devil. Why? "For God was with him."

You see, Ruth was not alone either. Her toil was very fruitful (John 15:5, 21; 1 Corinthians 15:56). Ruth was to glean. She was not reproached. One translation (verse 16 RSV) says, "And also pull out some from the bundles for her, and leave it for her to glean and do not rebuke her." So there was fruitful toil. In the 21st chapter of John, verse 10, Jesus said to the disciples, "The fish which you have caught." So you see, we can be fruitful in our toil.

John 15:5 says, "Without me ye can do nothing." 1 Corinthians 15:58, "We labor not in vain in the Lord." That's good, isn't it? We aren't working for nothing. Ruth got 55 pounds—an ephah—10 times more than she needed. I think that all of us can say since we've started to serve the Lord—that we've gotten more than what we needed. This was ten times…this bushel and three pints—fifty-five pounds, was enough. One omer—the tenth part of an ephah—was enough for one man, but she got 10 times more than what she needed for the day's wages.

God wants to do this for us! If the farmer didn't believe in this he would have quit a long time ago. He doesn't plant one bushel of grain and expect a bushel back; he expects it to come back in abundance. If he didn't do that, he couldn't stay in business. This is also the way it is with the church. The church is really a business institution, too, and a lot of people never want to invest anything in the church, however, we've got to invest to get back.

Ruth got 10 times more than what she needed…and she took all that he gave her. We have to get to that place in our experience. She left the straw and she took home the wheat. And so, when you're given something, thrash it out. If it doesn't pertain to you, leave it on the floor—it's straw—and take home the wheat! Some sermons have more straw than wheat.

And so, we see the tables are turned. God's hand is not against her now; it never was. She kept fast to her redeemer until the end. When you look at Ruth you see she was in heathenism; the tables turned for her now, and good is coming. And Naomi, the tables are turned for her as well.

GLEANINGS FROM THE BOOK OF RUTH

REVIEW QUESTIONS FOR CHAPTER 2

1. In chapter 2, what is Ruth doing?
2. What does the word "kinsman" mean?
3. The word "Boaz" means what?
4. When Ruth gleaned in the field, what did she do?
5. If we have a need, what do we do with Jesus?
6. Where was Ruth's place of service?
7. What does the word "cleave" mean?

CHAPTER 3
Ruth Is Resting

Naomi urges Ruth to claim her kinsman rights (verse 1): "Then Naomi, her mother-in-law, said unto her, My daughter, shall I not seek rest for thee that it may be well with thee?" Notice the difference in attitude here. When our heart gets right with God we have a different attitude about things. In the first chapter of Ruth (verse 9), notice her attitude: "The Lord grant you that you may find rest." Now Naomi isn't willing to find rest for her daughter-in-law. She said, "You go find it." And, she's going to send her to the heathen to find rest. Now, returning to chapter 3, verse 1, we read: "My daughter, shall I not seek rest for thee...."

Let me say, you can really tell the spirituality of people and their attitude about others. Some think they have to shut themselves up in a room or convent and think about themselves to be spiritual, when our attitude toward others is what really denotes how much spirituality we have. Naomi didn't have any spirituality in chapter 1, verse 9. She was a backslider. She was out in a foreign country away from God, but now she has returned and her attitude has changed. She says, "My daughter, shall I find rest for thee that it may be well with thee?" That's concern for others. We need to have concern for others.

Naomi was a Hebrew woman and she knew the custom. Ruth must press her claim. How did we get a redeemer? We pressed our claim. What is that claim? "All that come to me I will in no wise cast out." You pressed your claim when you said "Lord, you said you would save me, and I believe you're going to do this. Lord, you said you would heal me, and I believe you are going to do it. Lord, you said you would fill me with your Holy Spirit, and I believe that you can do it. Lord, you promised to supply all of my needs, and I believe that you can do it," but we've got to press the claim. And here is Naomi, a

Hebrew woman who knew the custom, so Ruth must press her claim. It was the poor who needed a redeemer, and God's law provided for a kinsman redeemer.

There's going to be a marriage here. Here's a little quote I want to share with you: "A man is restless while he misses his rib that was taken from his side; and the woman is restless until she gets under the man's arm from whence she was taken." This is only natural; that's the way God made us. So marriage is the settlement of all the problems of a woman. She has a husband and a home—these are things a woman desires. Ruth had hard struggles. She had widowhood. She needed protection. She desired headship. She had fruitlessness, and she was restless, tossed to and fro.

Ruth is a picture of us as well. We had hard struggles. Do you remember how it was before you served the Lord? We longed for rest. "Come unto me all ye that labor and are heavy laden, and I will give you rest." But don't stop there. "Take my yoke upon you and learn of me…and you shall find rest unto your soul" (Matthew 11:28, 29). These are true rests we can enjoy. God treats us as individuals; he does not deal with masses. Verses in Matthew, Mark, Luke, and John show us very explicitly that Jesus deals with individuals.

Naomi, in this chapter 3, is a type of the Holy Spirit. She's the matchmaker who caused us to get acquainted with Jesus, our Boaz—the Holy Spirit. We really became acquainted with the Holy Spirit before we became acquainted with Jesus. You see, He has to convict us and show us our need. Naomi, the matchmaker, is going to work things out, put it together. She's going to claim her rights with Boaz, and she gets Ruth a husband out of it, so really, isn't she a matchmaker?

Let's read a little more. Verse 2 says, "And now is not Boaz of our kindred, with whose maidens thou wast? Behold he winnoweth barley tonight in the thrashing floor." This word "winnoweth" means to toss grain so that the chaff—dry grass and straw (that which was worthless) would blow away. They would take oxen and put them on a tread mill, then they would tread out the grain. They had a post in the middle and they would put these oxen tied with a rope on it. They would march them around and around and as they went round and round the grain (kernels) fell out of the barley. They then would take a fork and whirl this up in the air against the wind and the wind would blow away the chaff. This is what Boaz was doing.

Boaz does the thrashing. It doesn't say the reapers were doing the thrashing; it says Boaz is doing it. We'd like to be in charge of the thrashing, but it's the Master. He will separate the wheat from the chaff. We are going to be pretty surprised on that day because some folks we think don't have anything are going to enter in, and some we thought had lots are going to be last. Doesn't the scripture tell us "the first will be last, and the last will be first"?

The thrashing floor here is a place of judgment—the place of separation of the chaff from the wheat. Then there is preparation for the wedding night. The harvest comes first, and then the wedding. The end of the age, and then the marriage of the Lamb. I think this chapter 3 is one of the most beautiful chapters in the Bible. It helps to show us what God is wanting to do in this age in which we are living.

Let's look at the preparation (verse 3). It, in fact, applies to everyone who is a believer in the church. There is a preparation—the equipment to come into His presence. Look at 2 Corinthians 7:1 (it is addressed to us who are believers), "Having therefore these promises dearly beloved, let us cleanse ourselves." Who does it? We do! We want the Lord to do everything. We ask Jesus, "Why don't you do this for me?" There are some things we have to do for ourselves. "Let us cleanse ourselves from all filthiness of the flesh and spirit." There is some filthiness in the flesh and filthiness in the spirit—notice, this is talking about believers. And this cleansing is to be a cleansing from all filthiness of the flesh and spirit, "perfecting holiness in the fear of God." So, we are in the harvest, and we must wash. The Lord is looking for pure people: "Blessed are the pure in heart, for they will see God" (Matthew 5).

Now the wedding is coming at the end of the age. First, we have a harvest. We're working now in the harvest field, and the wedding will come. You know how fussy everyone is about our earthly weddings. We think that the Lord will take anything, that it doesn't make any difference, but He wants a spotless people. The Lord says, "Man looks on the outward appearance," and that's true, but I want you to notice what God chose. He didn't pick some funny-looking person—even though He looks on the heart. It says that David was handsome and of fair countenance. He didn't pick out any bad-looking thing; he picked out someone that looked nice. We're not going to a funeral, we're going to a wedding, and this wedding is at the end of the age. The Lord wants to anoint us!

That's the next point here, "anoint us with oil." This is a picture of sanctification and of the infilling of the Holy Spirit. Notice what Naomi told Ruth to do: the bride gets ready. "Wash thyself therefore, anoint thee." In other words, put some perfume on, smell nice, get anointed! And you know, when we are anointed we have a perfume about us.

"Anoint thyself, put thy raiment upon thee." "Raiment" in the Word of God speaks of our conduct. We have to have conduct that is above reproach. "Let thy garments always be white."

"There are a few in Sardis who have not defiled their garments; they will walk with me in white." So we have raiment—the wedding garment.

And then there was humility. "Get thee down to the floor." This is humility. And then she was to "make not thyself known unto the man until he shall have done eating and drinking." The phrase here is "uncover his feet" (verse 4): "It shall be when he lieth down that thou shalt mark the place where he shall lie and thou shalt go and uncover his feet."

Let's look at Isaiah 60:13. This is a very good verse. This is a place of humility. We are to be there—"uncover his feet." "The glory of Lebanon shall come unto thee, the fir tree, the pine tree and the box together, to beautify the places of my sanctuary: and I will make the place of my feet glorious." We have an old song we sometimes sing, "Sitting at the feet of Jesus." We learn some things there you won't learn in seminary, you won't learn from a book. He will teach us some things at His feet. "I will make the place of my feet glorious."

This is the equipment now to come into His presence. There is a covering of righteousness. It's down in the thrashing floor. Even though there is going to be judgment and a separation of the good from the bad in our lives, He will receive us. In fact, I have a verse that I have enjoyed and it's something I've never seen in this light before, until I studied the Book of Ruth and God directed me to it: Isaiah 53:11. "He shall see the travail of his soul and be satisfied." What was his travail? To bring many sons to glory. And what will he be? Satisfied. "When my soul is resting in the presence of the Lord, I'll be satisfied." We used to sing that. In this, the third chapter, we see that Boaz is satisfied with the harvest.

Here are the instructions that Naomi (who is a picture of the Holy Spirit) and the Holy Spirit have given us to be ready for the wedding…to be ready for His coming:

- We must wash ourselves.
- We must have a wedding garment on.
- We must be anointed with the oil of gladness.
- We must be humble.
- We must uncover His feet.

Let's go over verse 4 again. "And it shall be, when he lieth down, that thou shalt mark the place where he shall lie, and thou shalt go in, and uncover his feet and lay thee down: and he will tell thee what thou shalt do." Where are we getting our instructions from? The Bridegroom. "He will tell thee what thou shalt do." Jesus knows what we are to do. He guides us. "Where He leads me I will follow."

Notice verse 5, and it would be good for us to get this into our thinking. "And she said unto her, all that thou sayest unto me I will do." Ruth said this to Naomi. Ruth is a picture of us; Naomi is a type of the Holy Spirit. How are we to respond to the Holy Spirit? All that He tells us to do, we will do it. John 14:16: "He will guide you into all truth." He will not speak of himself; he will show you things to come. That's good!

Verse 6 claims the benefits of the kinsmen. "And she went down unto the floor, and did according to all that her mother-in-law bade her." The word "bade" means "told her." That's an old English word; we don't go around saying that somebody bade us do something...it has lost it's meaning. This is what I get out of this passage: she is after the lover himself. The Bridegroom is better than barley. Ruth is not satisfied with barley; she wants Boaz.

It's time to ask this question, "Are you satisfied with what the Lord has given you so far?" Or, do you want Him? I want Him. I will not be satisfied nor rest until I get Him. I am so glad for the peace He gave me. I'm glad for the joy He gave me. I'm glad for the anointing of the Holy Spirit that He gave me. I'm glad for divine healing that He gives me, but I'm not satisfied; I want the Lover Himself!

One could compare it to the excitement over the engagement ring. Is the girl excited to just have the ring? She's crazy if that is all she wants. She's after the one who gave it to her. Likewise, we are not in love with the gifts He gave us, we get excited over the lover Himself.

Ruth is after the lover, Boaz. She risked all on Boaz. She expected him to do the part of a kinsmen—which he did. She trusted him implicitly or she would not have ventured to the thrashing floor. Understand, our salvation isn't complete yet. Christ saved me from the initial sin that I received from being a son of Adam. He saves me yesterday and today by sanctification, by the Word, and prayer. I'm separated not by the clothes I wear or the places I don't go to, I'm sanctified by the Word of God and prayer. Tomorrow I'll be saved, for I will be like Him, for I shall see Him as He is. Salvation comes in three installments: I can proclaim today I am saved, but I am saying this in faith that when He comes I will be like Him.

Now Ruth is pressing her claim. She risked all on believing that Boaz was going to do for her what he was able to do. This kinsman had to be related to the human family by blood. If it's Adam's blood in his veins, he's disqualified. Look at Hebrews 10:5, "Wherefore when he cometh into the world, he saith, sacrifice and offering thou wouldst not, but a body hast thou prepared me." You see, Christ had to have human blood to be a Redeemer. "Without the shedding of blood, there is no remission for sin." So, the kinsmen had to become a relative of ours. When Jesus was in heaven, he was not a relative of ours, but he became identified with us through taking on himself human flesh, being born in the womb of Mary.

Jesus was not made in the womb of Mary, He was the only begotten Son of God. He just used this channel through which to come into the world. You and I were made in our mother's womb, but not Jesus. Jesus is the begotten Son of God. He always was, but he was a spirit and spirits couldn't save us— a body had to save us, a body with blood in it and the blood now cannot be related to us. If it was Adam's, man or woman, he'd have the same blood you and I have, but you see, the blood line always comes from the father, and Joseph was not his father, "they supposed him to be." Joseph was not the father. Jesus did not get his blood from Joseph; he got it from his Heavenly Father. We believe in the virgin birth, and believe it strongly because the blood that saved us could not be Adam's blood.

As an illustration, let's use an old farm illustration. You can build a hen house as big as the church and put five hundred hens in it and get them all laying eggs, but you won't have any babies until you put roosters in there. It takes the rooster to bring production, and it's the same way with Jesus. He was born of the Virgin Mary, but he was conceived by the Holy Ghost, and he was not made in there; he used the channel for which to become related to the human family. He didn't take our sin, he wasn't born in sin nor shaped in iniquity. We get this from this verse. Ruth relied all on Boaz. She expected him to do the part of a kinsmen—which he did. She trusted him implicitly or she would not have ventured to the thrashing floor. She is after the lover, himself; the bridegroom is better than barley. While I'm grateful for the gifts Christ has given me, they are nothing compared to what it will be like when we get Him. You can't love prophecy, you can't love tongues, you can't love wisdom or knowledge, but you can love the Savior. We're after the Lover, Himself.

So Ruth went down and did according to all that her mother-in-law bade her. And then (verse 7) "When Boaz had eaten and drank, and his heart was merry...." I often think of kids with their parents when I read this, how after supper they will ask Dad if they can do something. As a child, if I asked Dad before supper it was always no, but if I waited until after supper I got away with a few things. But we all feel better after we've eaten. You see, Boaz had been thrashing...a pretty dirty, hot, sweaty old job. I don't know if I would have wanted anything brought up to me until I had washed and enjoyed a lovely supper or dinner. Ruth waited...that is what Naomi told her to do.

So Boaz had eaten and drunk, and his heart was merry, and he went to lie down at the heap of corn. The King James Bible is putting corn in there; however, it was the barley harvest that he was thrashing. Then it says, "and she came softly and uncovered his feet and laid her down." Verse 8: "And it came to pass at midnight that the man was afraid and turned himself; and behold, a woman lay at his feet." And in verse 9 it says, "Who art thou? I am Ruth, thine handmaid. I am your handmaid for thou art a near kinsman." She wanted to be covered by his righteousness.

Covered by His righteousness is a good place for us to be. At His feet, covered with His skirt, covered with His righteousness. We don't stand in any of our own righteousness today. Our righteousness to the Lord is as filthy rags. We need the covering of him... "for thou art a near kinsman."

Acts 2 says, "I will pour out my Spirit upon all flesh: and your sons and your daughters shall prophesy, and your young men shall see visions, and your old men shall dream dreams: And on my servants and on my handmaidens I will pour out in those days of my Spirit." Isaiah 28:12, "This is the rest that causes the weary to rest; and this is the refreshing." Verse 11 says, "With stammering lips and another tongue will he speak to this people."

Ruth was in need of redemption. She was alien, a widow, a Moabitess, needy, bankrupt, hopeless. We were needy, bankrupt. We didn't have a thing as far as God's Kingdom is concerned; hopeless. All these type us.

And Boaz said (verse 10), "Blessed be thou of the Lord, my daughter." Yesterday he identified with her and called her a daughter, and today he reiterates this. "...for thou hast shewed more kindness in the latter end than at the beginning, inasmuch as thou followedst not young men, whether poor or rich." There was quite an age span here. Boaz was in Elimelech's generation. Elimelech could have gone to Boaz but instead he went to the heathen for help. So now Boaz is an older man. He's in the age bracket of Ruth's former father-in-law, and now he's going to skip his generation and marry a young woman.

"Now my daughter, fear not" (verse 11). Do you know God's favorite word? Check the concordance for "fear not." It appears hundreds of times in God's Word: 364 fear nots! His word to us when he found us was, "Fear not."

And so Boaz said, "...fear not; I will do to thee all that thou requirest: [In other words, he was saying, I'm going to do everything that you need. Our Savior has done this for us.] for all the city of my people doth know that thou art a virtuous woman." Ruth was not after him for his physical appearance. Likewise, we have not seen our Lover [Christ]; we don't love him for his physical appearance, we love him for who he is and what he's done for us.

"And now it is true that I am thy near kinsman: howbeit there is a kinsman nearer than I." It was the nearest kinsman that could redeem the property and buy back all the inheritance. Is Jesus our nearest kinsman? No, we were children of somebody else before we were children of God. We were first His.

"Tarry this night and it shall be in the morning, that if he will perform unto thee the part of a kinsman well; let him do the kinsman's part; and if he will not do the part of a kinsman to thee, as the Lord liveth, lie down until the morning" (verse 13). We're resting until the morning. Boaz is going to wait 'til morning to see whether this kinsman was asked, Will you buy back the property of the Elimelechite? He wanted the land but he didn't want the individual. We find that to be a picture of Satan, who comes to rob, and to kill, and destroy. He wants everything he can get out of us but he doesn't want to do anything for the living.

He told Boaz, "I'll take everything but the woman. I don't want her." Again, a picture of Satan. He had you in his clutches and would have loved for you to be a slave of his, bound by his bondages, but the Lord set us free. He bought us back.

So it says, "Lie down until the morning." This is a picture of the church; we are lying at His feet until morning. We are gleaning until sunset and lying down until the morning. We are children of light, living in the dark, waiting for morning to come. There are children of darkness out there. They are living in the dark and they are blinder than bats! They think the Republicans or the Democrats are going to get them out of their dilemma. Our hope is not in the works of darkness; we're waiting for morning to come...King Jesus! "I am the light of the world; he that follows me will not walk in darkness." Thank you, Jesus.

Ruth "laid at his feet until the morning," and I like what follows, "and she rose up before one could know another." That's pretty early! And he said, "Let it not be known that a woman came unto the floor" (verse 14). This was a disgrace (in this culture); the woman's place was at home raising babies and cooking and cleaning. This woman was at the threshing floor, and she got out of there before day break.

Verse 15: "Also, he said, bring the veil." This can be translated "sheet" or "apron"...that thou has upon thee, and hold it. And when she held it, he measured six measures of barley and laid it on her." Notice, she got more for resting than for working! She received three measures yesterday for working and now six for resting. Ruth received more for resting than she did for working.

If three measures weighed fifty-five pounds, she got 110 pounds! Now look, "he laid it on her." She must have been very strong to carry this home. Could you carry 110 pounds? We picture Ruth being some little petite thing, but she must have been a little hefty to carry 110 pounds home.

Let's look at numbers again. Why wouldn't she have gotten seven? She got six. Six is the number of earth. It's the number of man. Seven is the perfect number. Barley was measured until she got Boaz and then she gets him without measure. We don't get all of the Holy Spirit. There are some who say they have the "gift of wisdom," however, there isn't such a gift. It's only a word of wisdom—we only get a word from God. If we had all His wisdom, no one could stand to live with us! We are getting things in measure. We are children of earth. We get six measures now, but in the morning we are going to get him without measure.

Notice, Ruth didn't go from his presence empty. He laid it on her, and she went into the city (verse 15). "And when she came to her mother-in-law, she said, who art thou, my daughter?" It actually means, "How did you fare? What happened? Reiterate it to me; tell me what's been going on."

"And she told her all that the man had done to her." What's that? Testimony time! When Jesus does something for us, we've got to bring up what He's been doing for us.

Verse 17: "She said these six measures of barley gave he to me; for he said to me, Go not empty." And it says, "She said, sit still, my daughter." This is hard for us. We think we have to be doing something to be ready, but it is the Lord that makes us ready through His Holy Spirit. If we will rest…and let Him lay "six measures of barley" on us, He will finish the bargain in the morning. When He comes, He's bringing it to culmination.

Naomi said, "Sit still my daughter until thou knowest how the matter will fall: for the man will not be in rest until he has finished the thing this day." Another picture of our Jesus today. He is at the Father's right hand. He doesn't know the day or the hour that He's coming for us; it's been reserved in the Father's hands, but He will not have rest until He brings His sons to glory. He is going to bring it to a culmination. He's not going to let it hang. What He starts, He finishes. He is not going to be at rest until He brings this to a culmination. He's not going to leave this world in a dilemma; He died to bring it to peace. You think He's going to be satisfied to have war? He won't be satisfied until His will is done on earth as it is in heaven.

REVIEW QUESTIONS FOR CHAPTER 3

1. In this chapter, what is Ruth doing?
2. Naomi is a type of what?
3. In this chapter, who is Ruth after?
4. What do we need to do to prepare for the wedding?

5. When Ruth went to the threshing floor, what was she in need of?

6. Ruth got three measures of barley for doing what? She got six measures of barley for doing what?

7. What the significance of the number six?

CHAPTER 4
Ruth Is Rewarded

The Hebrew word for "kinsman" is "goel." We've talked about "kinsman," and we've talked about "redeemer." These two words are synonymous. Twenty times "goel" appears in the Book of Ruth. In these four short chapters, it is used 20 times. Twelve times in the King James Bible it is translated as "kinsman," and nine times it is translated as "redeemer." They both mean the same thing; I have a kinsman, I have a redeemer.

In the New Testament sense we never really use this word, but this is what Jesus became for us—He became near of kin. He became identified with us. You see, He was a spirit in heaven. He was the second person of the trinity, but to save us He had to shed blood, because without the blood, there is no forgiveness. "Without the shedding of blood there is no remission of sin" (Hebrews 6, 9, 22). So there had to be blood shed, and Jesus didn't have any. God said somebody is going to have to go, and Jesus said He would go. Then He had to become identified, so He took the route of coming just like you and me, except He didn't have any blood line from an earthly father. His blood did not come from Joseph; it came from His Father, through the Holy Spirit. We were made in our mother's womb. We were shaped in sin and in iniquity, but Jesus was not like this. Jesus was born from the womb. He came that route to become identified with us. He didn't have any sin, and He didn't have any blood that came from Joseph or from a human father, so He became near of kin.

There's a verse in Hebrews (2:14) that says, "He took part." We must always remember that Jesus "took part." He didn't take all of us; He took part of us. He didn't take our sinful nature, but He became sin for us—it was laid on Him. Ruth had some things laid on her; Jesus had some things laid on Him for us. "Thou art a near kinsman," the kinsmen redeemer. God became kin to us. He chose kinship with us.

Now, let us look at the word, "redeem." When I say, "I will sing of my Redeemer," what do I mean? The word "redeem" in the Biblical sense means "to put back." Don't consult Webster's Dictionary for this meaning; you need a Bible Dictionary. God's intention was that all of us would be His children, but there was a day when Adam decided he didn't want to be His child. So, in rebellion, he became identified with Satan, and he became the child of Satan. You and I are first Satan's children, and through an act of new birth we become the Lord's children.

This causes some rumblings in some camps, because some believe that because a man and woman are believers and have a child, that child is automatically a sweet child of God. It is not! Until children come to the age of accountability, they can't enter into the kingdom, because where there's no knowledge of sin, you can't repent. You see, they are not born of God. God takes them because they have no knowledge of sin. You can't repent until you know you have done wrong. You can't really repent until you say I've done this, and I'm sorry for it; that's repentance.

To redeem Israel—according to the Old Testament law of kinship—the nearest of kinsmen relatives had the right of redemption. To put back, to re-purchase property and persons, and to raise up the name of the dead. If the brother died without issue, his brother would marry the widow and raise up the name of the dead.

In the case of Ruth, Elimelech died. He didn't have any brothers, so Naomi couldn't get a husband. The two sons they had both died and left two widows. There were no other children, so there was nobody that they could go to and press the claim and say, "You've got to take me," because there were none. Boaz lived in Bethlehem, and when Naomi came back, she decided to get this Moabitess girl to press her claim. He is near of kin to us; press the claim.

We press the claim when we are saved. We don't get saved by sitting and wishing. We must press our claim. It's "Ask and you receive, seek and you will find, knock and the door is opened to you." That is the only way He works. He isn't going to work your way, He's got a way He's going to work. How important do we think we are that we are going to tell God what to do? You are going to do what He's outlined to do, and then you'll have certain things. That's the way He works.

Turn to Leviticus 25:47. I had a lady tell me one time that if the Book of Acts was taken away from us Pentecostal people we couldn't live. If I have only Leviticus I would be able to stand for everything I believe. We have salvation in Leviticus—what else do we need? There is healing in Leviticus. It talks about the King that is coming in Leviticus.

Here in verse 47 we find the law of the kinsman, the redemption of servants. "And if a sojourner or stranger wax rich by thee, and thy brother that dwelleth by him wax poor, and sell himself unto the stranger or sojourner by thee, or to the stock of the stranger's family: after that he is sold he may be redeemed again" [that word means bought back, to put back, or buy back]: "one of his brethren may redeem him" [that means a kinsman, a relative, and Jesus became our relative to buy us back]. What was lost in Adam we get back in Jesus. Adam came and gave me death, and sin, and transgression. Now I get everything back he took from me, in Jesus. What I lost in one I get back in the other.

Verse 49: "Either his uncle, or his uncle's son may redeem him, or any that is nigh of kin unto him of his family may redeem him; or if he be unable, he may redeem himself." This is the Old Testament Law. We can't redeem ourselves. He could—if he got prosperous enough—because it was earthly money.

Verse 50: "And he shall reckon with him that brought him from the year that he was sold to him unto the year of jubilee" [that's the 50th year]: and the price of his sale shall be according unto the number of years, according to the time of an hired servant shall it be with him. If there be yet many years behind, according unto them he shall give again the price of his redemption out of the money that was bought for. And if there remain but few years unto the year of jubilee, then he shall count with him, and according unto his years shall he give him again the price of his redemption. And as a yearly hired servant shall he be with him: and the other shall not rule with vigor over him in thy sight. And if he be not redeemed in these years, then he shall go out in the year of jubilee, both he and his children with him. For unto me the children of Israel are servants; they are my servants whom I brought forth out of the land of Egypt. I am the Lord your God" (verses 50-55).

That is the law of the servant, the kinsman's rights. This is God's law provided for kinsmen. You see, only the poor needed a redeemer. That is why we need one—we are poor. Now when we say poor, don't think about what you have in your purse or in First National Bank—think very poor otherwise. It is talking about all the things that we lost. We lost a lot more than a pocketbook in Adam. This body is wracked with pain, and sin, and strife, and disobedience, and lust, and idolatry, and all these things came because of what Adam did for us. In rebellion he walked out on his Maker, but Jesus died to bring us back. This is what the redemption business is all about.

Perhaps this will help you gain an understanding of redemption. The pawn broker holds the article until the redemption ticket is presented. The ticket gives us the right to redeem within a specific time. If within the stated time you get enough money, you can go back down to the pawn broker and give them the money and take back your article. But in the meantime, if somebody comes in and has money and wants this article, your article is gone, and your ticket doesn't amount to a hill of beans.

This is a picture of what Jesus did for us. He walked in and paid the price. He has a down payment on us—He has not redeemed us yet. He has put down the down payment. He called it the "earnest" of the inheritance. He gave us His Spirit, and now He's going to come back to redeem His people.

The Savior walked in, sometime on Sunday, because Sunday morning He said to Mary, "You don't touch me. I haven't ascended yet to my Father." But He went there and laid His blood on the altar [mercy seat] of God. He laid his blood there and then came back. Because He came back He said, "Now you can handle me; you can see who I am because I've done this for you. The purchase agreement has been completed, but you and I haven't had the redemption of our bodies yet—that's coming! So, He has a down payment on us and what He's done, He's able to perform—this is redemption.

Now let's go through the places where this "goel" appears. Read Ruth 4:13-14. These are places where this word "goel" appears. Genesis 48:16 says, "The Angel which redeemed me from all evil, bless the lads; and let thy name be named on them, and the name of my fathers Abraham and Isaac; and let them grow into a multitude in the midst of the earth." Notice that the word "Angel" is capitalized. There are few places in the Bible where angel is capitalized. This is the blessing of Jacob now upon his sons, and he blessed Joseph and said, "God before whom my fathers Abraham and Isaac did walk, the God which fed me all my lifelong unto this day...." You see, our Savior appeared in Old Testament times as the Angel of the Lord. This was Jesus pre-incarnate. He took upon him the body of an angel and appeared to Jacob, to Israel, and to Joseph (verse 15). That word in verse 16 is "goel" for "redeemer."

Exodus 6:6 has another example: "Wherefore say unto the children of Israel, I am the Lord, and I will bring you out from under the burdens of the Egyptians, and I will rid you of their bondage and I will redeem you with a stretched out arm and with great judgments." Now this is what the Lord did for us. Egypt is a type of the old life. This verse 6 says, "Wherefore say unto the children of Israel...." We are children of Israel; that's another name for Jacob. He was a surplanter and a crook, and his name was changed. Do you remember when your name was changed from crook, and a surplanter, and a deceiver? We had a name change. I think of the song, "There's a new name written down in glory...and it's mine, O yes, it's mine!"

"I am the Lord, and I will bring you out from under the burden of the Egyptians." Don't you want to get out from under the burden of the Egyptians? If we seek Him first and His kingdom, all these other things come as a matter of due course. "And I will rid you out of their bondage and I will redeem you with a stretched out arm, and with great judgments."

The third example is in Exodus 15:13. "Thou in thy mercy hast led forth the people which thou has redeemed...." It's the Lord who saves us. "Thou hast guided them in thy strength unto His holy habitation." We are not home yet, but He has us started on the way, and we have great assurance that He's going to finish this that He started.

Example four is found in the Book of Job, one of the oldest books in the Old Testament. If we had our books in chronological order we would have Genesis, and then Job. There is nothing in Job that has a word about the law in it, so Job lived in the days of Abraham. I marvel when I read the Book of Job over all the light God gave him. Job 19:14: "My kinsfolk have failed, and my familiar friends have forgotten me."

We mentioned this before. When it comes to Ruth, the first kinsman was not Boaz. Boaz was number two. The first one wasn't willing to do it because all he wanted was the land; he didn't want the woman. This, we saw, is a picture of Satan. We were first children of Satan, and he wanted everything we have. He robbed us, he stripped us, he left us for dead by the side of the road, but he didn't want us. His only interest in you is to destroy you.

So the first man was not willing, and since he was not willing, the responsibility came to number two. Salvation is always in the second person. You can read the whole Bible through, and you will find "salvation" means "deliverance" and is never in the first person. Adam...it wasn't in Adam, it was in Christ. It is also found in the story of Cain and Abel, Esau and Jacob, and many others.

There are churches that try to tell us we were all nice and loving. We weren't...but we shall be! Job 19:25 states: "For I know that my redeemer lives and that He shall stand at the latter day upon the earth." You see, our kinfolk have failed, and my familiar friends have forgotten me, but Job assures us, "I know that my Redeemer lives!"

Example number five is in Psalms 103:4, "Who redeemeth thy life from destruction; who crowneth thee with loving kindness and tender mercies." He redeems—or buys back. He buys us back from our life of destruction.

The sixth example is in Psalms 107:2: "Let the redeemed of the Lord say so, whom he hath redeemed from the hand of the enemy." If you're redeemed you are supposed to tell about it; say so!

Example seven: Proverbs 23:11, "For their redeemer is mighty; he shall plead their cause with them." The redeemer is mighty! This word can be translated as "strong." Aren't we glad that we have someone to plead our cause? When you were little and did something wrong, remember how a brother or a sister would go along with us to Mom and Dad and plead our cause. It seemed to make the punishment much easier.

Example eight: Jeremiah 50:34: "Their redeemer is strong; the Lord of hosts is His name: He shall thoroughly plead their cause, that He may give rest to the land, and disquiet the inhabitants of Babylon." This is a picture of the old life—Babylon. When we look at the children of darkness, this is really what they are coming to. There is confusion and unrest, and they are in division over what's coming to pass.

Example nine: Isaiah 35:9, "No lion shall be there, nor any ravenous beast shall go up thereon; it shall not be found there: but the redeemed shall walk there." (Verse 10) "And the ransomed of the Lord shall return and come to Zion with songs and everlasting joy upon their heads: they shall obtain joy and gladness, and sorrow and sighing shall flee away." The redeemed are coming home with singing! This characterizes God's people.

Example ten: Isaiah 49:26, "And I will feed them that oppress thee with their own flesh; and they shall be drunken with their own blood, as with sweet wine, and all flesh shall know that I, the Lord, am thy Savior and thy Redeemer, the Mighty One of Jacob." In the King James Bible, notice that "Savior," "Redeemer" and "Mighty One" are capitalized. These are blessed names of our Savior. "All flesh shall know." And what does it say in Acts 4:12? "There is no other name under heaven given among men whereby we must be saved." Paul writes that in Philippians 2, "Every knee will bow and every tongue will confess that He is Lord."

"All flesh shall know that I, the Lord, am thy Savior and thy Redeemer, the Mighty One of Jacob." When we read these Old Testament words we think of the twelve tribes, but you see, we are spiritual sons and daughters of Jacob; we have become spiritual. The wild branch as been grafted into the tree [the olive tree], and we have become sons and daughters. We may not look like Jews, but we are spiritual sons and daughters of Jacob.

Example eleven: Psalms 51:10, 22, "Create in me a clean heart O God; and renew a right spirit within me. Cast me not away from thy presence; and take not thy Holy Spirit from me." In this verse we have "goel" mentioned, even though Redeemer has not come. The words "O God" can be translated "goel," my Redeemer.

Example twelve: Isaiah 52:9, "Break forth in joy and sing together ye waste places of Jerusalem: for the Lord hath comforted his people, he hath redeemed Jerusalem." Jerusalem is a picture of all three citizens. We "live in Jerusalem;" we have been freed. We once lived in bondage—we were in sin—and the Lord brought us out and to Jerusalem. We are free citizens living in Jerusalem…and he says, "He has comforted his people, and he has redeemed Jerusalem." You don't "live in Jerusalem" if you aren't redeemed.

Example 13: Isaiah 54:5, 8, "For thy maker is thine husband; the Lord of hosts is His name: and thy Redeemer, the Holy One of Israel. The Lord of the whole earth shall He be called." (Verse 8) "In a little wrath I hid my face from thee for a moment; but with everlasting kindness will I have mercy on thee, saith the Lord, my Redeemer." This gives reference to when darkness covered the earth, and God turned his face and his back on His Son. He said,

"I hid my face for a moment in wrath, but with everlasting kindness will I have mercy on thee, saith the Lord, thy Redeemer.

These are good verses where "goel" appears. Then we have it in the New Testament in Hebrews 2:14, 15, "Forasmuch then as the children are partakers of flesh and blood, he also himself likewise took part of the same; that through death he might destroy him that had the power of death, that is, the devil. And delivered them who through fear of death were all their lifetime subject to bondage." Notice in verse 14 that He only took part of it. We have to remember that He had flesh, and He had blood, but He didn't have any sin. His blood was special blood; it was blood from His father. It was created by the Heavenly Father; it was not the blood of Adam. Jesus took the fear of death out of us. It's good night here and good morning up there! "To be absent from the body is to be present with the Lord."

In the Old Testament light, we need to understand…Ruth is going to come and press her claim to the man. She has gone down to the floor and uncovered his feet and laid there. He was startled when he woke up and found a woman lying at his feet. Wouldn't you be startled? A strange woman came to the threshing floor, and there she uncovers his skirt and lays herself down. Awaking around midnight, he found a strange woman lying there and said, "Who are you?" He knew her—he was just startled and surprised to see her there. And she said, "I have come, and I want you to do the part of the kinsman for me." And he gave her six measures of wheat. She got more for resting than she did for working. So, when you are resting before the Lord, don't think you're not getting anything. You are getting twice as much as you are out there shaking the bushes!

Let's look at the qualification of the Redeemer. There are three things the Redeemer has to do; not everybody could redeem. First of all, he must be a blood relative. He must be the nearest relative, but he could not be involved in ruin. In other words, I might be the nearest relative, but if I didn't have anything and was pennyless, I couldn't help one who was also pennyless. Satan worshipers say nothing about a redeemer because Satan cannot be a redeemer; he's involved in ruin.

This teaches us that we were first slaves to sin. Our Master was involved in ruin. Jesus (the "goel" of our perishing race) was not a kinsman by nature, but through grace (that's unmerited favor) he placed himself in a position where he could be our kinsman and do the part of a kinsman. He became the Son of man. You will not find this in the Old Testament. He became the Son of man after Matthew, chapter 1. He became identified with us. In addition to being the Son of God, He became the Son of man. He did this to bring us in. It was grace that did this—unmerited favor. Related, but not in ruin, because He had no sin. He was the seed of a woman.

Let's read John 8:46, 47, some wonderful verses that Jesus gives us: "Which of you convinceth me of sin? And if I say the truth, why do ye not believe me? He that is of God heareth God's words: ye therefore hear them not, because ye are not of God." The Pharisees and the Saducees wanted to point an accusing finger at him, but He said, "Which of you can convince me of sin?" He didn't have any sin, though he was the seed of a woman. He was God and man veiled in flesh.

The "goel" must be free himself, not implicated in man's sin. John 14:30 says, "Hereafter I will not talk much with you: for the prince of this world cometh, and hath nothing in me." Some will try to tell you that the virgin birth is no big deal. They have gone so far as to say Mary lived in the red light district of Jerusalem, and Joseph was a soldier stationed there. He had an affair with her, and they had a baby out of wedlock, and this made her a terrible thing. The Bible says, "She never knew a man." The virgin birth is a big deal. We are not saved but for the virgin birth, so that is a big deal.

The second point is that he must be able to redeem. Boaz means "strength;" he had power and wealth (Ruth 2:1). "And Naomi had a kinsman of her husband's a mighty man of wealth...." That's the only place you'll find God's Word saying that about another person. The kinsman must have the price of redemption, the right to save the least, the lost, and the last...and that's our Lord Jesus.

Boaz could pay the price. He had lots of land, he had lots of money, and he probably had lots of cattle even though it doesn't say anything about it. Boaz redeemed with silver, and Jesus redeemed with His blood. He paid the price to satisfy the justice of God. There could be no redemption unless there was blood—God says that in His Word. He said to the children of Israel, "Without the shedding of blood there is no remission for sins."

There was no angel that could come and redeem us; angels didn't understand. Angels are only peering into what's going on; they are ministering spirits to the hearers of salvation. Let's not get them doing a bunch of other stuff. If God sends one or more to help, that's fine. If he sends two to help, fine; I don't see them. And if they are helping—and I hope they are—they can do a little bit more! We don't want anything to mar Jesus in our presence with the power of the Holy Spirit. So, it took blood to redeem us. The only way this could happen is that God's Son took upon Him the likeness of man, and He came to earth to redeem us.

We have seen that he must be able and a blood relative, and the third thing is he must be willing. Some people are related, some are able, but there are many people that are not willing. Let's look at this now from the Word of God.

The nearer kinsmen was not willing. Ruth 4:6 says: "The kinsman said, I cannot redeem it for myself, lest I mar mine own inheritance...." Let's take that out of its setting for a moment and look at Satan himself and tell him he is a great big liar. That's just the way he thinks about us. "I can't help them, I'll mar my own selfishness." We know explicitly that Satan cannot do it for us.

The first part of verse 6 sounds so sad because he doesn't want to "mar my own inheritance." Jesus was willing: "Lo, I come to do thy will." and "Not my will, but thy will...." There was no compulsion. Hebrews 10:7 says, "Then said I, lo, I come to do thy will, O God." This is also a quotation from the Book of Isaiah. We see that Jesus met all the qualifications of the redeemer. He became identified with us through blood. He was able to do this, and he was also willing.

Let's review the duties of the redeemer. The first thing that must be done is redeem the persons. He must redeem the persons who had sold themselves into slavery. They were sold under sin, and they needed release, and the price paid in full. This man must pay all the debts. Naomi and Elimelech left his land. Ten years went by, and taxes had to be paid. They are now into their eleventh year. Eleven years of bondage and debts, and the redeemer would be willing and able to pay all the debts and get them out of the dilemma they are in. Jesus did this for us, paying sin's debts. The price for our redemption is the precious blood. (Ephesians 1:7; Romans 5:14; Romans 6:14; and Romans 8:2.) He was willing to pay the price to redeem us back.

Duty number two is he must buy back all the property. Every Israelite had an inheritance; all of us have an inheritance. Jesus died to give us our inheritance. People are interested in what they are going to get from their parents. They become afraid a brother or sister is going to take it away from them. I'm more interested in my eternal inheritance. Let the devil know that you're getting everything you have coming to you—and sell out to Jesus. The devil doesn't want you to get your inheritance. Jesus died and became a kinsman. The Bible contains the sealed evidence of His purchase. His wounds are the open evidence that He paid the price.

The world is in alien hands. Satan has this world in his hands; man lost it through sin. Study Luke, chapter 4, regarding the temptation of Jesus, and you will find all that the devil has. He has this world in his hands. Satan, the prince of the power of the air, is the spirit that is now working in the sons of disobedience. 1 Peter 1:4-5 says: "To an inheritance incorruptible and undefiled, and that fadeth not away, reserved in heaven for you, who are kept by the power of God through faith unto salvation, ready to be revealed in the last time."

The third claim is redemption. The subject of the Book of Ruth is redemption. Redemption by blood and redemption by power. "Raise up the name of the dead." He must redeem the person, buy back all the property, and raise up the name of the dead. If you were a woman married to a man, and he died, you would go back to his brother and ask him to take you in because he is the nearest kin. This is why they said to Jesus, "Now this woman was married to this man, and he died, and she looked up his brother, and he died. And she looked up another brother, and he died, and he had seven brothers; last of all she died."

The point I'm trying to bring here is that there were seven men. She was married to all of them because she was trying to look for a redeemer to redeem her out of her problem. The redeemer—the kinsman—had to raise up the name of the dead. So when Boaz marries Ruth and they have a child, he can't call the child by his last name; he has to call it by the dead man's name. That could take some pride away from you! Here Boaz has a lovely son by this Moabite girl and she has to give credit and evidence to the dead man. We don't do things unto men—we do them unto God. The kinsmen had to have his motives in the right place. He had to love the dead more than the living. Think about that for a while! Naomi and her husband's name was cut off through death, that his name be not blotted out. God is greater than death, and a barren Moabitess widow was brought into the royal line.

Notice in Matthew 1:5: "And Salmon begat Boaz of Rachab...." This is the genealogy, and there in this line in Matthew are five women, four of them are names that people would leave out of a family tree. And then, "Obed begat Jesse..." that's the father of David—King David. So here's a poor little Moabite, a heathen from a land of darkness, who comes into the genealogy of Jesus. God used all of this in His plan. What does it teach us? Though we were bad—awful—He brought us in as sons and daughters, and yes, we are in the royal line today.

Salvation is always in the second person: we have the first Adam, and we have the second one, Jesus. We have Cain, who killed his brother, and we have Abel. We have Esau, who sold his birthright, and we have Jacob. It is always in the second person. Allow this to whet your appetite to trace through the scriptures and see what one person did and what the relative did after them, for this teaches us that our salvation didn't come in what we were born as; it always comes in what's happening next. We've all had a natural birth, but it takes a spiritual one. It always comes in the second person. This is clear all through the Word of God that the Lord brought us in...He's the Redeemer.

"Then went Boaz up to the gate and sat him down there: and, behold, the kinsman of whom Boaz spoke came by; unto whom he said, Ho, such a one! Turn aside, sit down here. And he turned aside and sat down. And he took ten men of the elders of the city and said, Sit ye down here, and they sat down! And he said unto the kinsmen: Naomi, that is come again out of the Country of Moab, selleth a parcel of land, which was our brother Elimelech's: And I thought to advertise thee, saying, buy it before the inhabitants and before the elders of my people. If thou wilt redeem it, redeem it, but if thou wilt not redeem it, then tell me that I may know: for there is none to redeem it beside thee; and I am after thee, and he said, I will redeem it." (Ruth 4:1-4)

Ruth 4:5: "Then said Boaz, what day thou buyest the field of the hand of Naomi, thou must buy it also of Ruth the Moabitess, the wife of the dead, to raise up the name of the dead upon his inheritance."

Every nation has its own domestic laws or rules; and among those prevalent in Israel was the relationship of the goel. He was the redeemer, or the next kinsmen of the one deceased, whose duty it was to purchase an inheritance in danger of terminating.[1] These duties were defined in the

Levitical law. According to the Law, the kinsman was expected to marry the widow of the deceased and to raise up seed unto the dead, and also to buy the property. It is evident from the Book of Ruth that both of these duties were centered in the same person.

So Boaz goes to the gate of the city where the ritual of kinsman is carried out.[2] Here, there are ten men who were judges, who sat ready to apply their wisdom to this problem and act as witnesses to the transaction. The nearest kinsman wanted the land, but not Ruth. So to Boaz (who was next in line) fell this responsibility. He was not only able, but also willing to complete the transaction.

Ruth's acceptance and redemption by Boaz was the reward of her integrity, service, and commitment. You see, steadfast service and commitment will lead to an everlasting reward. In other words, it brings blessing. Boaz had been impressed by her life and work. She had made herself worthy of acceptance by him. Her willingness to sacrifice her desires in order to be of service to Naomi had won Ruth great respect.

In a book called *Rules from Ruth*, the author, W. G. Heslop, wrote, "Self-sacrifice is self-saving and self-sanctifying. Self-seeking and self-loving is self-destruction." Orpha went back to Moab, to her people, and to her gods…and we don't hear of her anymore. But Ruth counted the cost, paid the price, sanctified herself—and she stands honored and exalted among the Old Testament saints.

Remember, Ruth is a type of the church. This theme is observed from Ruth's poverty and loneliness in chapter 1, to her conclusion in Boaz's redemptive act in the later chapters. Then, remember that Boaz is a type of Christ, who is our kinsman-redeemer, the principle we looked at in chapter 3. In verse 13 it says, "So Boaz took Ruth, and she was his wife: and when he went in unto her, the Lord gave her conception and she bare a son."

In the joy of their union, a child is born. There is no greater joy, no more precious gift, than the gift of life. Verse 13 says, "and she bare a son." Look at the end of the chapter, in verse 17. "Then was a son born to Naomi, and they called his name Obed: he is the father of Jesse, the father of David."

The name "Obed" means "a servant."[3] It is a reminder of duty. We should never despise service. In fact, as Christians, we are to be "meet for the Master's use." We are not placed where we are to serve selfish ambitions and plans; we are here to serve the King of Kings and Lord of Lords.

Ruth probably didn't realize that this son, Obed, would be the link to the continuation of the family that would eventually bring the Messiah (v. 22). What God pledged in his covenant to Abraham was confirmed in the covenant to David.

The story of Ruth closes with happiness and hearty congratulations. Naomi, whose trials and sorrows began at the beginning of the book, have changed to renewed happiness: her daughter-in-law, a mother, she herself a grandparent, is surrounded by rejoicing neighbors, expressing their congratulations and invoking blessing upon her and those close to her. The story loses sight of Ruth in picturing the happiness of her mother-in-law. Verse 17 says, "There is a son born to Naomi," but in verse 14, it says, "Blessed be the Lord, which hath not left thee this day without a kinsman." So we see Naomi encompassed with the blessings which should accompany old age, "honor, love, obedience, and a host of friends."

Naomi's unselfishness is finally rewarded.[4] Naomi had all along thought more of Ruth's sorrows and of Ruth's happiness than her own. And now Ruth is made the means of her prosperity, comfort, and joy in her last years. Naomi's hopes are fulfilled. It was Naomi's desire that Ruth might attain to "rest." And now she sees the Moabitess a happy wife and a happy mother. This grandchild becomes the joy of her life, "a restorer of her life," and a nourisher of her old age. The child, Obed becomes her delight and her imaginations picture his manhood and his position in an honorable line of descent.

The Book of Ruth closes with a genealogy, which we see in the Book of Matthew. Matthew's genealogy bears the name of Ruth, a foreigner in the royal line of the King of Kings. This is important because when Ruth made her choice, "Thy people shall be my people, and thy God, my God," she became a vital part of God's purpose and plan.

What we see with Ruth is a commitment borne out of true concern to serve God and others, which is a rare virtue among people today, and even among many Christians. Forgetting self for the benefit of others is not a simple thing to do, but it is important to full commitment.

The greatest honor given to Ruth is that she was brought into the ancestors of David and Christ; this Moabitess woman, and through a kinsman-redeemer, was brought into the royal line…and there is no greater honor given to us than for the "sinner to be saved by grace" and to become a part of the family of God. An old hymn says, "I was once a sinner, but I came, pardon to receive from my Lord...."

Paul, the apostle, writes in Romans 8:17, "Now if we are children, then we are heirs—heirs of God and co-heirs with Christ, if indeed we share in his sufferings in order that we may also share in his glory."

What a wonderful truth to know that through our Redeemer, Jesus Christ, we have been brought into the family of God.

REVIEW QUESTIONS FOR CHAPTER 4

1. What are the qualifications of the kinsman-redeemer?
    (a)
    (b)
    (c)
2. What is the Hebrew word for "kinsman"?
3. What does the word "redeem" mean?
4. Egypt is a type of what?
5. The price for our redemption was found in what?
6. In chapter 4, Ruth is rewarded. In what way?
7. Ruth is a type of what?
8. The name, Obed, means "a servant." What does this remind us of?
9. What was the greatest honor given to Ruth?

NOTES

[1] *Pulpit Commentary*, Chapter IV, v. 22, p. 69, vol. 4.

[2] *The Adult Teacher,* Gospel Publishing House, 1980, p. 96.

[3] *Pulpit Commentary*, p. 71, vol. 4.

[4] *Pulpit Commentary*, p. 71, vol. 4.